Lingering Lessons on Life & Leadership

Learning from our lifetime soulmates.

CONTENTS

Dedication	5
Foreword	7
Introduction	9
Lingering Lessons	11
One	13
LEAD	23
Companion	31
Courage	37
Sing	43
Three	47
See	55
Band	59
Whole	63
Friend	67
Today	73
True	79
Certain	85
Thread	89
Measure	93
Better	99
Conclusion	105
Lorenzo	107

DEDICATION

This book is dedicated with great love, respect and appreciation to my precious father-in-law, Noel Cromhout, whose outstanding example, ongoing care and profound wisdom over decades helped me in immeasurable ways to become the leader I am today.

FOREWORD

I have had the pleasure and honor of knowing Lorenzo, Delray and their fantastic children, Bianca and Joel, for nearly thirty years. Lorenzo is a master communicator who immediately disarms and inspires you with his authenticity, humility and humor. He has a unique approach to helping people position themselves so that they can benefit by seeing their life, situation and strengths from a refreshing perspective. His story and the lessons you will glean from these pages will build insightful mile markers into your journey and help you not only reflect on your life but adjust your approach with a sense of joy and anticipation!

Lorenzo's global life experience has shaped his genius to bring light, love and latitude, which I'm sure will apply to you irrespective of your vocation, passion, culture or experience. He loves to help people discover keys that open doors to new vistas while instilling courage to step across the threshold into those new opportunities.

You will be inspired and challenged to embark on a journey of learning that will release the full beauty of who you are irrespective of where you are at this juncture in your life. Enjoy, linger, learn and lead!

DJ McPhail, Leader of Liberty Global

INTRODUCTION

Thank you for purchasing this book. It has taken over thirty years of life and learning to be in a place where I could finally put some important lessons down on paper. My hope is that you will find great encouragement, freedom, and help in these pages.

I chose this title because it represents a profound and inescapable truth: there are some lessons we learn over the course of our lifetime which come around again and again. As you grow through experience and hopefully gain wisdom, the second and third time they visit you they are deeper and higher and broader and more powerful. Like old and trusted friends, they take up residence in your mind and heart, and when most needed, appear at just the right moment to help you make important decisions and choices. It is these lingering soul mates we explore in this book.

Each chapter has one main thought, idea or lesson running through it. My goal is to then explain how or what I learned from the particular lesson and what it has meant for my life and leadership. Sometimes I share information or anecdotes I have read, but mostly I use my own life experiences as these force me to be authentic, courageous and practical. To make the material accessible and digestible, I have intentionally used everyday conversational language as if we are sitting opposite one another chatting over a meal. Although this is not strictly a study book, there should be much to learn in what you read. The chapters are not arranged in any particular order. There is no plan to follow. You may want to read the book in one sitting or a chapter at a time, with breathing space in-between to absorb what you have gleaned.

I would encourage you to pause and meditate on any thought or story which touches and challenges you. I always find it helpful at arresting moments to temporarily put down the book, close my eyes, and imagine a picture in my mind of what I have just imbibed. This usually takes me to other places in my heart, mind or soul, and I then find it easier to recall the material at a later date.

This is not a book offering simple fixes to life and leadership problems. It is a river to swim in, and as the water flows over you, I pray it can refresh, encourage and strengthen you in your own life as a leader seeking to bring glory to God whilst doing good to others. Life is immeasurably precious. Lessons we learn and add to our essence are gifts to be treasured for eternity, and it always pays handsomely to linger for a time on both.

Lorenzo Agnes

LINGERING LESSONS on LIFE & LEADERSHIP

Lingering

To remain or stay on in a place longer than is usual or expected, as if from reluctance to leave; to dwell in contemplation, thought, or enjoyment.

Lessons

Something from which a person learns or should learn; an instructive example; a useful piece of practical wisdom acquired by experience or study.

Life

The period of animate existence of an individual; a corresponding state, existence, or principle of existence conceived of as belonging to the soul.

Leadership

The ability to influence others to action.

ONE

Psalm 139:13,14

"For you created my inmost being; you knit me together in my mother's womb. I praise you because I am fearfully and wonderfully made; your works are wonderful, I know that full well."

It is fitting that we begin our journey with the most important life lesson discussed first: you are unique. Psalm 139 in the Holy Bible perfectly details and explains our Father's heart toward us and His intentions for us. As the Scripture so beautifully puts it, He has wonderfully made each of us. It is appropriate language because everything God makes is truly wonderful - literally, full of wonder - as it is His own doing. It is impossible for us as sinners, with our clouded understanding, to fully grasp the endless goodness of God toward us when He carefully, intentionally and lovingly wove us together in our mother's womb. Meditate on this majestic revelation for a few minutes: you are unique. Intentionally created by God. There is only one of you. You will never be repeated. Ever. This truth is wonderful, humbling, frightening and exhilarating.

You have been created to be and to do what no other human being ever can or must and it is within this framework we approach the writings in this book. God has unique expectations of our uniquely crafted life. We have responsibilities we alone can and must fulfill, which if neglected, will never be satisfied. This knowledge is an almost impossible weight to carry without the grace of God enabling and guiding us. It is an eternal joy to live out and the true privilege of life.

It makes sense then that the single most significant gift you can give God and this world is to properly and fully express your God given uniqueness.

Recently I celebrated thirty years of marriage to Delray, a most amazing woman, my wife and life companion. Our children, Bianca and Joel, are now adults and remain the people we are closest to and love more than anything in this world. Also, I have very dear friends spread around the globe who love and respect me with honesty and dignity. I could not be who I am and where I am today without these crucial relationships in my life. The most important truth in all of this is that they learned to love and accept me for who God made me to be, even if at times I disappointed them. They have enjoyed, celebrated and unlocked God's uniqueness in me, with encouragement to express it fully and freely. Those dearest to me have understood the need and power of living your uniqueness.

Unique. A beautiful concept. A wonderful truth. A powerful reality. Now if what I said above is true, we then have to answer life's two most important questions: who am I and what am I here to do? Some find the answers to these questions early on in life, but for most of us, they take many years to discover, let alone understand and live out.

To celebrate and communicate this God-given revelation, I created a LifeSpace called LiveUniq. LiveUniq is based on a radical, powerful premise: that every human being is created by God for a unique purpose, and this purpose is woven into the very fiber of our being by a loving Creator whilst we are growing in our mother's womb. Typically, we as adults view a newborn baby as a blank sheet of paper on which we "write" to prepare it for the best possible future. In our homes, churches and schools, we have built complete systems for imprinting and shaping the lives of children in order to equip them for life. This is not wrong or bad, but I think it is based on limited understanding and can be unsatisfying in terms of ideal effect. I firmly believe that in the nine months a child is being formed by God in their mother's womb, He places within it everything required for this unique individual to fulfil His unique God-given purposes throughout their lifetime. Parents, teachers and friends should be working together to properly understand who God has made us to be and what He created us to do within His great Plan. In essence, we must partner with our Creator to release all that He has placed in us, for His glory and for the benefit of all mankind. I call this process Unlocking. We all need to be unlocked much more than we need to be shaped.

My own life reads like a fairytale. What wasn't supposed to be, is. What was certain to happen, didn't. My personal story is a journey immersed in endless Grace. When I met Delray it was love at first sight for both of us, even as it seemed out of the realm of possibility that I could have this beauty for my life partner. We found each other in a small, out of the way church on a lovely Summer day and were married a year later. Over three decades, from the sorrow of apartheid South Africa to the joys of a progressive church in upstate New York, to a thrilling new mandate in Boston, our journey has been one of love, suffering, joy, pain, beauty, and significance.

Born in London of Italian parents, returning to Italy while an infant, and then crossing a continent to end up in South Africa as a small child, I grew up there before we eventually moved to the United States. British, Italian, African and American. Quite a blend but one for which I am deeply grateful, and in God's purposes, absolutely necessary. I love to tell people that I have a European soul, African heart and American spirit. As you can see, the Father's unique plan for my life is beyond anything I could have dreamed up!

I found God at twenty years of age and finally stepped into my Unlocking. It began with a deep, true personal relationship with my great Unlocker, Jesus Christ, and continues to this day. After completing a degree in Graphic Design at the University of Cape Town, South Africa, I entered the world of advertising and design, which I thoroughly enjoyed and within which stirred the beginnings of an adventurous life. A decade later, Delray and I entered full-time ministry within the context of the hateful, broken, beautiful nation that was apartheid South Africa, and from the very beginning, we knew there was something different about our union. Even as a child I always had a sense of destiny deep within my soul. Often accused of being too much of a dreamer, there was a quiet longing for the new, the better, the greater. Once Delray and I came together, destiny became reality and took shape in accordance with His great intentions. From serving with our fellow suffering Christians in the townships of Johannesburg to serving with our friends in the slums of Bangladesh, we are living testimony to the importance and joy of being unlocked.

You are created by a loving God. He has made you fully unique. You have a purpose no one else has or will ever have. My desire is that you will come to understand how, why and what it is you have been made to do. The word "unique" is defined in the dictionary as: being the only one of its kind; unlike anything else; particularly remarkable, special or unusual. From the Thesaurus: distinctive, individual, special, distinctive; single, sole, lone, unrepeated, unrepeatable, solitary, exclusive, rare, uncommon, unusual, sui generis; informal one-off, one-of-a-kind, once-in-a-lifetime, singular. Ok, we get the message: to be unique is something truly wonderful!

Let this reality sink in .. there is not, has never been, and will never be anyone like you.

You should feel loved, joyful and privileged at such wonderful knowledge. And you should also feel somewhat frightened, challenged and humbled by the responsibility of such a revelation. Think about this for a moment: if God made only one of you, would it not make sense then that you have been lovingly created by Him to fulfil very particular purposes in His immeasurably great plans which only you can accomplish? It is also true then that if you do not take the time and trouble to find and release your God-given uniqueness, you and the whole world will miss out and be incomplete.

I was raised at a time in the world's history when the generation before mine would say to us: don't ever think you're indispensable! We can easily replace you! There are plenty more where you came from! Such untruth .. such lies .. such nonsense! The Scriptures are very clear that our loving God takes great pains to create and celebrate each one of His unique creations. The Bible tells us He has a name for each of the trillions of stars in the night skies. Do we really believe that God would celebrate the uniqueness of a simple star and not delight immeasurably more in the uniqueness of each child He forms in their mother's womb? Are we not His highest creation, made in His own image? The beautiful fact is we are totally indispensable! By His intention and according to His design! You can never be replaced! No, you are not one in a million – you are the only one among billions. These words are not designed to make you feel good about yourself. They are written to help us humbly appreciate the individual responsibility we carry to be all He has created us to be, finding our purpose and fitting into His great, eternal plans for mankind.

This book is about living out your God-given uniqueness. And to do that we have to make the time to discover who He made us to be and what He made us to do. When we find our uniqueness, we must free it and allow His Holy Spirit to form us so that we can flow in the grace and power of the life He has designed for us. I can this process UnlokU. God put into you in your mother's womb everything you need to serve Him and His purposes throughout your whole life. Psalm 139 plainly and clearly tells us that He knows every day of our lives before we live one of them. The Bible also makes it very clear that our God is fully sovereign. He knows all things from beginning to end, so this gives us the freedom and courage to obey His will for us. We rest in what He has decided and designed!

The Bible also tells us that we are all born sinners and that without His forgiveness and grace in our lives, which comes through accepting His one and only Son Jesus Christ as our personal Savior and Lord, everything we do brings death. So I ask you: how can a perfect, loving, all-powerful God entrust His awesome creation - you and me - into the hands of sinners? Does it not make much more sense that He, the sovereign Lord who knows all things, would put into you in the nine months you are in your mother's womb what He knows you will need for the rest of your life? Yes, that is more correct. A baby coming into the world is not like a blank sheet of paper we must "write on" to shape its life. The miracle of a child is the creation of an almighty, all-knowing God who has uniquely created this life to serve Him all the days of its lives. Our task as parents, family, and friends is to work together in harmony with the Holy Spirit to understand who the Father has made this unique life to be and what he has created them to do. And all along the way to partner with God and one another to unlock the nature and purposes of God in the life He has blessed the world with.

This is perhaps the most significant lesson I have learned so far in life: *expressing your God given uniqueness is the most important thing you can do with your one life here on earth.*

LEAD

Romans 12:8

".. he who leads, with diligence .."

Essentially, leadership is the ability to influence to action. It is getting others to surrender their time, treasure and talent in order to facilitate your vision and accomplish your goals. It is invisible, yet tangible. Elusive but manageable. Often as much art as science. What we do know for sure is that almost everything rises or falls on leadership.

Over many years of leading myself, my family and several churches, I have come to the conclusion that leadership can be best understood as having four key elements: love, example, attitude and discipleship. An easy way to remember these is that the first letters of each word form the acronym LEAD. The Bible says that God looks at our hearts in order to see who we really are. When He finds a heart like His, He favors that individual's life. The Scripture also tells us that out of the overflow of the heart, the mouth speaks. In other words, who we are instructs what we say. Both of these truths have to do with our motivation, and motivation for doing something is almost always the key to success or failure in God's Kingdom. With this in mind, let's look at the four key elements necessary for a life of God honoring, effective, and fruitful leadership.

Love
You are a Shepherd: this is your Motivation.

1 Peter 5:1-4
"To the elders among you, I appeal as a fellow elder, a witness of Christ's sufferings and one who also will share in the glory to be revealed: Be shepherds of God's flock that is under your care, serving as overseers—not because you must, but because you are willing, as God wants you to be; not greedy for money, but eager to serve; not lording it over those entrusted to you, but being examples to the flock. And when the Chief Shepherd appears, you will receive the crown of glory that will never fade away."

1 John 3:16&23
"This is how we know what love is: Jesus Christ laid down his life for us. And we ought to lay down our lives for our brothers. And this is his command: to believe in the name of his Son, Jesus Christ, and to love one another as he commanded us."

Love is the foundation of the Kingdom and it is the life-blood of all service to God. Sometimes I hear leaders say, "I love serving God, and I like the ministry.. it's just the people I have no time for", and my heart is saddened and offended because the main reason they should be leaders is their love for people. Whether you're a church minister, business person, school coach or military sergeant, if your essential motivation for leading is not the love of people, you can never fully accomplish what God expects of you. In practice, leading by love is very hard work. As we see in Jesus' life, everything He did was motivated by love, yet He was abused, disrespected, hated and eventually murdered. But He also was loved, respected, appreciated and followed. Love brings all of these with it because it is at once a balm and a fire. It is our deepest motivation.

Example
You are a Teacher: this is your Responsibility.

Titus 2:7,8
"In everything set them an example by doing what is good. In your teaching show integrity, seriousness and soundness of speech that cannot be condemned, so that those who oppose you may be ashamed because they have nothing bad to say about us."

Many years ago the Lord showed me this jarring reality: everything you do teaches something to someone. At first, I was excited by this revelation, but soon it began to scare me as I realized how true it is. As a teacher - a living example - your leadership demands a constant awareness of your responsibility to God and people to live in such a way that He is glorified and they are helped. It requires a huge dose of humility and willingness to be held accountable: first by God, then by yourself, and then by those in authority over you. Accountability is very important, and I thank God that from when I was a new Christian, I have always had fantastic examples of humble servants of God who submitted themselves to being taught by fathers and mothers in the faith with spiritual authority over them, willingly taking the responsibility for being living examples themselves. One of my "secrets" to "success" in the ministry is having these examples to follow and imitate, the most powerful one being my father-in-law.

Attitude
You are a Servant; this is your Practice.

1 Corinthians 4:1,2

"So then, men ought to regard us as servants of Christ and as those entrusted with the secret things of God. Now it is required that those who have been given a trust must prove faithful."

Under-rowers all are we! In the original Greek language, the word used for "servants" is also translated "ministers", and in this verse it means "under-rowers", referring to slaves who were rowers on Greek ships of war and commerce. Paul is comparing ministers - leaders - to these men. Some of these ships would have two or even three levels of rowers, all straining together to the rhythm provided by the beating of a huge drum for them to row in unison. They would be beaten by guards screaming at them to row harder and faster. As they bled from the whip lashes tearing the skin off their backs, the strain would be too much and their hearts would burst in their chest, killing them instantly. Their bodies would simply be thrown overboard and a fresh slave would take their place.

Paul the Apostle is comparing ministers to under-rowers! Not only rowers, but those on the lowest, most brutal level of the ship. His point is that this must be our attitude as leaders as we serve Christ and His body. Our heart must be to do whatever it takes to move the "ship" of His Kingdom forward, even if it costs us our dignity and freedom. As you can imagine, leadership in the Kingdom is not for the faint of heart. Note that in the verse above, it doesn't say that those entrusted with God's Kingdom must be successful: it says they must prove faithful. Faithfulness is first an attitude, then a series of choices, and then a way of living.

Disciple
You are a Worship Leader: this is your Purpose.

Exodus 3:12
And God said, "I will be with you. And this will be the sign to you that it is I who have sent you: When you have brought the people out of Egypt, you will worship God on this mountain."

When considering all that the Israelites went through and witnessed of God's miracles to get out of Egypt, it's amazing to me that the first thing God requires of Moses as a leader is not some spectacular act but to lead His people to meet with Him face to face, as Moses himself had experienced years before at the burning bush in the desert. This speaks volumes about God's priorities for His people. Moses was required to lead God's people to His mountain - into His presence - where they could encounter, hear His voice and experience His power for themselves. This is, in fact, the greatest privilege and single most important purpose of Kingdom leadership. Even Jesus' main task was to bring people back into relationship with His Father.

Every time God's people gather for a worship service, it is the leader's first and main purpose to bring the congregation to the place where they are personally and communally before God, hearing His voice for themselves, as they worship and glorify Him in love and truth. Everything else is secondary. It is possible to have an exciting, superbly organized church service and not meet God at all .. just ask the Pharisees.

As leaders, when we bring God's people face to face with Him, He transforms them into His disciples. As we see in the account above, it is impossible to meet Him, hear His voice, see His power and come away unchanged. Whatever else you do as a leader, this has to be your primary purpose.

COMPANION

2 Corinthians 13:14

*"The grace of the Lord Jesus Christ, and the love of God,
and the communion of the Holy Spirit be with you all.
Amen."*

This powerful verse reveals how the Trinity communes and works with us. Jesus relates to us personally through His perfect grace, whilst the Father showers us with His love and the Holy Spirit, through intimate communion, gives us daily instruction and guidance. What a stunningly beautiful reality. The Holy Spirit speaks to us, builds community with us and connects us .. all the time! Another way to understand this is that the Scripture tells us that He continually walks with us "closer than a brother".

What does "closer than a brother" mean? What does it look like? How does it work? Until we understand that everything in God's Kingdom moves through the Holy Spirit, and then accept Him for who He is, we cannot serve God properly or effectively, let alone powerfully or completely.

Misconceptions regarding the Holy Spirit abound. Some think of Him as a "force", a "power" to be called upon for "special tasks". Some people are even afraid of Him and unsure of His true identity and purpose. Others consider Him unreachable. Our opinion of God's Holy Spirit must be based on the Word of God and His truth, not on second-hand fears, misunderstandings or ignorance. The way to guarantee fruitful and effective leadership in life and ministry is having the Holy Spirit as your constant companion: leader, teacher, counsellor, enabler, guide and friend. This is how God designed His Kingdom to flourish and function - through His Holy Spirit.

I was raised a Roman Catholic and had no understanding regarding the Person and purposes of the Holy Spirit. He was a distant "it", some kind of power to avoid and even be afraid of. He was, in essence, a completely unknown in my very shallow and ill-defined Christian faith so typical of an average twice-a-year Catholic. However, two months after I was miraculously born again just before my twentieth birthday, I received the Holy Spirit into my life in greater measure when I was baptized into Him according to God's Word. I immediately burst out speaking in tongues as He enabled me, with tremendous joy overwhelming my spirit and soul. At that same moment, I was supernaturally healed of a back ailment and He has been faithful to walk with me daily ever since. Although I knew hardly anything of the Holy Spirit,

I immediately felt a profound closeness to Him and have found it completely natural to live in a state of constant communion with Him since that glorious night.

When you feel accepted by God's Spirit and are able to speak with Him openly, it brings you into a state of spiritual confidence and freedom. It is so much easier to learn from life and to serve in ministry when He is your constant companion, guiding your steps and correcting your mistakes. I am not saying that I live in a way that never pleases Him or causes Him to seem distant because of course I still sin and make awful choices which affect our relationship. But, when I feel His displeasure, by God's grace, I can immediately ask His forgiveness, repent, and have our friendship is restored.

Everything - and I mean everything - done in God's Kingdom here on earth, in the name of Jesus and for the Father's glory, is done through the Holy Spirit. Once our Lord Jesus Christ had completed His ministry on earth and ascended to Heaven to be seated at His Father's right hand, the Holy Spirit completely took over His roles and responsibilities to bring God's Kingdom on earth. He now works with and through us, Christ's Body, to accomplish His Father's will and purposes. Remember that Jesus was born by the Spirit, raised by the Spirit, anointed by the Spirit, and performed all of His ministry in the power of the Spirit. He also was able to suffer through Gethsemane and the cross at Calvary by the

Spirit's power and enablement. If this was true for Jesus, how much more must it be true for us as His children?

Sadly, I have to say that the parts of the Church which today continue to ignore the Holy Spirit and His supernatural workings on earth have done a great disservice to themselves, their followers and this broken world. To put limits on the Holy Spirit in any way reveals a fundamental flaw in understanding the Trinity, the Bible, the Kingdom and the Person of the Holy Spirit. I pray God will be merciful in His dealing with those who push aside His Holy Spirit due to their own fears, folly or desire to be in control of their destiny. I strongly recommend that if you are a member of a church where the Holy Spirit is not warmly welcomed, openly embraced and fully followed, you should seek fellowship in a place of worship where He is the leader and not men or women seeking to have their own way in place of the Father's desires.

You may be wondering how one learns to walk closely with the Holy Spirit. It begins with fully believing and accepting what the Bible says about Him, and then consciously relating to Him through this understanding. Every revelation from God is accompanied by a corresponding responsibility. Think about it: when the God of the universe chooses to reveal something of Himself or His ways of working, it will cause us to glorify and worship Him, and also to want to live out that revelation. For example, as a young Christian, when the Holy Spirit first helped me to properly understand that I was completely forgiven of my sins through Christ's work on the Cross, it profoundly impacted my relationships. Suddenly, I had a deep awareness that as one forgiven, I had to now forgive everybody who had sinned against me. Further on in my journey, He also showed me that to be a fruitful leader for God, I had to live free of unforgiveness otherwise I would always be leading from a place of weakness and incompleteness.

Once you learn to live by Who the Scriptures reveal the Holy Spirit to be, you also begin to relate to Him in a very natural, organic way, just like you do with any friend you know, love and trust. Because as we know, He is not a thing or a power, He is a Person. He is an equal member of the Trinity and profoundly committed to us as children of God. He is our Teacher, Counsellor, Friend, Guide, and Enabler. You can think of Him as one of the great leaders you admire from a distance, whose books you avidly consume, hanging on every word, wanting to be just like them. Except that He is perfect, all powerful and completely trustworthy, and by some miracle we cannot fully grasp, dwells in us.

Speak to Him continually. He is your best friend after all. The Bible says He sticks closer than a brother. You can pray to Him, call out to Him, sing to Him, and just plain love Him. He is a perfect gentleman so will never intrude, but He will always respond if you communicate with Him. Usually, when I speak to people about the Holy Spirit like this, someone will ask me how I know He is speaking with me. It's quite simple really. He can speak with actual sound, where you hear an audible voice speaking to you, although this is typically quite rare. Usually, it's a thought that pops into your mind or heart. Sometimes it's a feeling or sense you get in a given situation. We have some direction for understanding how He communicates revealed in 1 Corinthians 12. There are nine manifestations (or expressions) of Him (referred to as "gifts") explained in this Bible chapter. (This is a much deeper discussion to be covered in another book of mine, God through You.)

So the lesson for us is this: as in any relationship, you get out of it what you give to and put into it. It's no different in our relationship with the Holy Spirit. You have to spend time speaking to Him, asking Him what He thinks about a situation you face, and then waiting to hear His response or direction. He loves you. He made you. If you have surrendered your life to Jesus Christ and are living for Him, the Holy Spirit will gladly share His life and power with you. He is wonderful, creative, gentle, kind, powerful, involved and majestic.

I pray you will make the decision today to focus your life on getting to know Him, *your awesome life companion*.

COURAGE

Joshua 1:9

"Have I not commanded you? Be strong and of good courage; do not be afraid, nor be dismayed, for the Lord your God is with you wherever you go."

In a conversation I once had with Malcolm Hedding, a powerful man of God and fine example of someone knowing what they were created to be and do, I asked him why it was that so many of the leaders in his generation had not accomplished what he and my father in law, Noel Cromhout (a hero of the Faith) had done. I was explaining my concern as a younger minister that my generation did not have many examples to look up to and follow. When he became thoughtful, Malcolm had this odd habit of rocking backward and forwards on the balls of his feet while rattling the coins in his pockets, which he was now doing. It was a lovely moment, and then suddenly, with a confident grin, he looked me squarely in the eye and said, "That is easy to answer my friend ... courage! We had the courage to do what God asked us to do!"

This became a life-defining conversation for me and Delray. We had become heavily involved in cross-cultural reconciliation ministry in South Africa at a time when it was unpopular and dangerous to do so, and many voices were cautioning us to give up on this cause. But we knew God had made us reconciler's, like His Son, and although it cost us friendships, income, and popularity, to this day we believe it was one of the most important seasons of our lives in Him. Although it was good to have the courage to stay true to His call, it required total obedience to go and do what was required of us.

I learned first-hand through this experience that courage is usually the differentiator between significance and obscurity, and the power behind the courage is obedience! When we are obedient to Christ's commands, we are in practice declaring that He is actually Lord of our lives and will do whatever He tells us to do, without questioning Him. This is why the Bible teaches that obedience is better than sacrifice. I can quite easily sacrifice some thing which belongs to me, but obedience to Him often requires me to sacrifice myself: my time, energy, money and dreams, for His glory and the good of others.

As I'm sure you have worked out by now, I am a firm believer in the idea that God has created each of us uniquely for a particular purpose. Although we all serve Him in many similar, general ways, I am convinced He has something for each one of us to do which only we *must* do. This is His mandate for your life requiring you to be obedient to what He has given you to do. It is *your* mandate, no one else's. You cannot exchange it or run away from it. You can choose to obey it or ignore it, but you cannot escape it. Some mandates take decades of preparation before the Father can place them in our hands to serve and fulfil. I have received one of these so I'd like to share my mandate story in the hope it will help and free you to be courageous and obediently live out your own mandate.

I spent the first ten years of my ministry life learning under three other leaders. I'd like to say it was an easy decade but there were many challenges and in some ways, I learned more of what not to do than what to do in the ministry. Each of the men I learned under taught me invaluable life and ministry lessons and I am grateful for them to this day. After ten years of struggles (mostly not the result of our own doing) and joy, my family and I took a church in upstate New York in the city of Schenectady called Calvary Tabernacle. We spent fifteen happy and fruitful years fulfilling this particular mandate, during which time I and the church grew enormously in the Lord.

From the beginning of my time there, the Holy Spirit began to open doors for me and the church to serve Him globally through mission trips and leadership conferences in various nations around the globe. The church was courageous and supported our vision wholeheartedly, and God granted us an effective leadership team as we obediently transformed the church's culture to mimic that of the Church at Antioch in Acts 11. We also became deeply involved in serving our local community through various ministry and culture initiatives - it was a wonderful time.

As much as our local work flourished, the Lord also a had a global mandate for me to fulfil. Under my leadership, a wonderful fellowship of like-spirited friends serving God's Kingdom around the globe became what is today the Shakaba Global Family, so I needed to travel even more than before to grow and shape this global community into a force for God's kingdom. Eventually, the Holy Spirit spoke very clearly to me and our leadership team that the time was approaching where He would require me to step down from leading Calvary Tabernacle Church to lead the Shakaba Global Family full time. It took two years of planning and preparation but eventually I stepped into my God ordained mandate.

As you can imagine, it took courage and obedience for someone at my stage of life and ministry to lay down what we had built and step into something fairly unknown, having now to forgo a predictable income and live by faith, fully reliant on God for everything as never before. To be frank, it some ways it wasn't hard to do. I knew in my spirit that God had spoken. I also knew from enjoying His faithful provision for thirty years that He would make sure we had what He knew we needed.

On a human level, it may have looked like a foolish decision to make and some of our friends even suggested I stay on at the church as a figurehead and fulfil my mandate from within the safety of a stable income. They were well-meaning because they love me, so I took no offence at their suggestions, but I knew by now that obedience is always better than sacrifice.

As a result, we suffered a combination of hardships, difficulties, delays, frustrations, joys, blessings and new opportunities. It's been hard work to make such a huge life adjustment, but we now each run our own business, live in a city we love, have made new friends and are enjoying a new measure of fruitfulness in our life and ministry together.

And I am most pleased to report that not only did He care for me and my family through this journey but the new mandate is in full swing and I am happy to be serving Him from a place of joy-filled obedience rather than comfortable sorrow.

Courage requires obedience and obedience has to produce action. When you know God has spoken, you need to take a step of faith and respond to His mandate for your life.

Better to struggle in the promised land than languish comfortably in the desert.

SING

Mark 1:14,15

*"Jesus came to Galilee, preaching the gospel of the
kingdom of God, and saying, "The time is fulfilled, and
the kingdom of God is at hand. Repent, and believe
in the gospel."*

I once heard Jack Hayford tell the story of when he met
the resident Minister at the White House who had been
a Pastor to several Presidents and asked him which
subjects he preached on. He replied that every great
preacher has three sermons in him and they're all on the
same subject. In my spirit, I was immediately aware this
was an utterly profound statement, and as I meditated
on this beautiful explanation, something incredible
occurred to me: God gives us each a Kingdom note to
sing, and we sing it all of our lives.

Imagine a conductor as he stands before the orchestra
conducting a great piece of music. Every time he points
to the violinists, they respond by playing the notes of
music set before of them. They wait for his instruction
and then react with perfect obedience, in perfect time,
at the correct pitch and intensity. I believe the Kingdom
of God works in a similar fashion. God puts what I call

Our "LifeNote" into us in our mother's womb. As we grow up we find ourselves singing (living) this note at first subconsciously, or naturally, though unintentionally, and then later, once we discover it, with clarity and a sense of purpose. As you look back over your lifetime, you see traces of it everywhere, even when you were not yet a follower of Christ, because it was always in you. Once I came to know Jesus Christ as my personal Savior and Lord, suddenly my LifeNote became much clearer to me and now I sound it with understanding and intention.

How do you know what your LifeNote is? There are several ways to tell but one of them is that you find yourself drawn to the things and people who resonate on the same frequency as you. When you meet them, you will know them. You sense it, feel it and then express it. Your instincts, desires and passions are usually powerful indicators, and the things in life which fulfil you and give significance to your existence are also important clues. Because God lovingly placed it in you in your mother's womb, you have been singing it already.

For example, you may find that there is a certain constant in you always manifesting, regardless of circumstance or people. As you look back, you notice that mercy has always mattered immensely to you. You're concerned about how people are treated, generously give money to the poor, always advocating for those who are desperately in need of restoration because they have been abused. Injustice revolts and angers you. You find yourself talking and preaching about mercy and how important it is for every human being. I would suggest your LifeNote is mercy.

In the Scripture quoted above, we see Christ's LifeNote clearly revealed: bringing the Kingdom of God on earth. All of His teachings, preaching and service flowed from and back to His Father's Kingdom. The result of Him singing His LifeNote was countless people coming to know His Father as He did. And the sound of His LifeNote continues to resonate to this day!

If we go back to the example of the conductor and the orchestra, we can say that the goal of the music served by the orchestra is to move the audience into an experience which affects them emotionally, intellectually and spiritually, and many composers used music as a vehicle for a particular message they wished to communicate. Similarly, in the orchestra of His Kingdom, God uses our LifeNote to communicate His love, truth and power to a dying world.

Once you discover, understand and develop your God given LifeNote, it frees you to "sing" for Him. Gone is the uncertainty and the constant wondering about your life purpose. The deep need for destiny is now satisfied and you can get on with the supernatural task of singing His song through your life.

THREE

Exodus 19:17

"And Moses brought the people out of the camp to meet with God, and they stood at the foot of the mountain."

As a leader of a congregation you have many and varied roles and responsibilities to fulfill. Actually, in a typical church, there are far too many things constantly demanding your attention. Until someone has actually been in the position of leading a congregation, trying to satisfy God's requirements and meet people's needs, it is impossible to appreciate or understand the pressures that come with the job. Although we can adjust and change our roles and responsibilities as we seek to adapt and be relevant to the constantly shifting landscape of local church life, I have found there are three essential roles every leader cannot avoid or surrender if they desire to honor God and truly help His people. Every leader has three main responsibilities: worship leader, kingdom resource manager and culture creator.

Worship Leader
Our first task is to take people from where they are and bring them face to face with the living God where they can hear His voice and know His presence for

themselves. It wasn't coincidence that Moses' first objective after delivering God's people out of Egypt was to bring them to a place where they encountered Him for themselves. He understood, at the deepest level, that when people met God they would be forever changed, just as he was when He heard God's voice and saw His presence at the burning bush in the desert. I knew that my highest purpose and goal as a Pastor and leader is to bring people to God so they can know Him for themselves. This is why our worship services were designed with this one main purpose in mind: that people would experience and meet with God in authentic and powerful ways.

How should we measure leadership? I believe it is according to how many people under our leadership have met God and are still serving Him in daily communion and obedience. Practically, I made a point every Sunday of opening our worship services by having everybody hold hands and focus on God, from the welcome greeting to the opening prayer to the worship. We regularly made opportunity for people to come down to the front of the church and fall on their knees before God, creating the necessary time and space for them to meet with their loving Creator in a deeply intimate manner. I can't tell you how many times people shared with me how God powerfully met with them and changed their lives during these experiences.

Kingdom Resource Manager

It is mind blowing when we consider the fact that the God of Heaven entrusts His divine, eternal resources into the hands of frail and sinful men and women. When the Holy Spirit revealed to me that my task in the church was to manage His resources in a manner that was Biblically correct and fruitful, facilitating our God given vision to bring Him glory, it gave me great joy and freedom but also caused me to shake in my boots. What a great responsibility! He has entrusted to me and our team *His* resources of people, time, treasure and opportunities in order to produce the fruit He needs us to produce. And to do so humbly, thankfully, generously, faithfully and fruitfully. This is an impossible task without His leading, His enabling and our courageous obedience.

Due to the reality that all of us who serve Christ the King are a part of His great Kingdom, this truth is applicable to churches, businesses, colleges, schools, etc. For example, if you are a businessperson, God has entrusted you with His resources to produce fruit for His kingdom to advance, so that many souls come to know and worship Him for themselves. You may be too busy to serve in a ministry in the church, but you can facilitate the vision out of your finances, experience and networks. Once we become conscious of this responsibility, it delivers us from the tyranny of strict budgets, service agendas, and long-term planning meetings. Instead, it frees us to step fully into His vision and direction, living being led by His Spirit with Kingdom fruitfulness and power.

You must identify, quantify and employ all of the Kingdom resources He has entrusted to your care. It takes humility, diligence, maturity and tremendous teamwork to get it right, but when you do, the results are astounding. One of

The ways I did this was to immediately make our leadership team aware of my own strengths and weaknesses and then surround myself with other leaders who have Kingdom gifts I don't possess in myself, in order for our God given vision to be fulfilled. I am a strong initiator but a weak completer, so I placed around me leaders who were good at finishing things I had started. In this very practical way, our vision was advanced at a level and pace we could never have achieved had I not understood that my role was to fruitfully manage the resources He has already provided.

Culture Creator

As I travel the globe speaking with leaders in varied situations, I am constantly reminded of the crucial role culture plays in the life and essence of a given entity, whether a family, church, business, school or club. When a visitor attends your church, they are unaware of your vision, policies, practices and don't know your people, so the thing they feel which will mostly determine whether they'll return or not is your culture. Culture is visible and invisible; tangible and intangible; obvious and not; strong or weak; valuable or cheap. When we consider that eighty percent of all decisions people make are based on their feelings, if you truly want to share God's love with them, you have to improve your "culture communication".

The fact is that the leader, more than anybody else, shapes the culture of an organization.

If a church has a leader that doesn't have a clue how to do this but is a wise Kingdom Resource Manager desiring that people meet God, he will facilitate others on his team to fill this role.

For example, at our church we had a very engaging, energetic Youth Pastor by the name Mark, a true Kingdom treasure and resource. After we realized that the weakest portion of our Sunday morning worship was the end of the service, I asked Mark to bring our time together to a close by having everyone do something communal and to do it in his particular style. Mark would vigorously bound up onto the stage, grab the microphone and with a huge smile encourage everyone to stand up, join hands and pray with him. Pretty soon, it became a part of our church culture that we greeted one another warmly at the beginning of worship and celebrated passionately at the close of the service. This "culture sandwich" ensured people soon adjusted their expectations in such a way that visitors always felt loved and excited to be a part of our community.

Our staff and church were friendly because I was. They were generous because I was. They were creative because I was. Our essence was prophetic because I was. As a leader, you cannot escape the reality that you shape the culture, whether it be conscious or unconscious. Your God-given gifts, personality, and life experience all combine to feed and shape your culture. I always say culture is a person, so be sure to shape who the culture "person" of your community is, because every time people meet you, they meet your invisible - yet tangible - culture person as well. They may forget your sermon or business plan, but they will remember what they felt because of your culture. And as the leader, you're the person most responsible for creating, shaping and expressing it.

A note on personality:
I have sometimes heard leaders declare, "Our church is not built on personality!" This is absolute nonsense and indicates a limited and shallow understanding of God, a poor grasp of Scriptural reality and ignorance of how the Kingdom works in real life. The fact is God has always built His Kingdom on earth through (not on) personalities, whether it be Moses and David in the Old

Testament or Jesus, Paul and Peter in the New Testament. God gladly gives us our personality as He lovingly and intentionally fashions us in our mother's womb, happily creating us to be the unique person He intends. Almost always, the people who make these kinds of comments have very little personality or charisma themselves. Typically, they're insecure, have poor social skills and rely on their intellectual and organizational abilities rather than their personhood to serve God's people.

Sadly, there is a great irony here: every human being has a personality and leads by that personality, whether it be loving, energetic and charismatic, or distant, lethargic and tiresome. Even the leader declaring that their church will not be built this way is in actuality building the church on or through their own personality, for better or worse. The only other option is to have a machine - with no personality - build God's church. It's just silly nonsense so please ignore it when you hear it.

You can tell I'm passionate about this! There are a couple of reasons for my intensity: firstly, there are many tremendous emerging leaders in God's Kingdom with inspiring personalities who have been squashed by insecure, unhappy senior leaders, thereby robbing the Church and the world of potentially powerful, fruitful gifts and abilities. Secondly, God happily gives us our personality and any leader who suppresses the person

God has created us intentionally to be is in essence saying to Him, "I don't like what You have created and will not tolerate it in my church!" These "leaders" diminish God's Kingdom, His people, and themselves.

Never apologize for who God made you to be!

SEE

Matthew 28:19

"Go therefore and make disciples of all the nations .."

Leading a church which over the course of several years became a wonderful, fruitful expression of God's kingdom, I learned early on that one of the most important things required of me by God was to seek Him for His vision for the congregation He had entrusted to my care. I was acutely aware that I was placed there by Him to help shape the church into the image He had originally designed for it from before time began. My God given work was to lead the church in such a way that they would become who God wanted them to be and to do what He had already ordained for them to accomplish.

Although every local church shares similar Biblical responsibilities, they also have a powerfully unique mandate, ordained by God, to fulfil. The leader's responsibility to God and the church is to understand what that mandate is and then to lead the church in such a way that they accomplish their God given purposes. A vision from God enables you to say, "Yes" to the right things and "No" to distractions. It clarifies and simplifies the way you spend your God given resources: people, money, time and opportunities.

When I arrived at Calvary Tabernacle Church, they had just been through a very painful split and the congregation was hurting, tired and insecure. Thankfully, the Holy Spirit visited us and we immediately found ourselves in a state of divine favor, enjoying God's gracious hand upon us from week to week. I have to say for the record that it had very little to do with any of us - it was as if He had chosen to favor us and that was that. Within the first two months, I had sought for and received from the Lord His vision for the church. It read like this: To be a Kingdom Resource Centre for Christ, Redeeming the Destinies of Children in Need. It was clear, specific and made us accountable to Him and to one another. It brought the church together around God's task for us, created unstoppable momentum, and released His resources into our midst.

We quickly blossomed from just over one hundred people to a congregation averaging eight hundred on a typical Sunday. He transformed us from an inward looking, hurting church to a fully outward looking community with a global footprint in missions, and most importantly, involved in our local community serving children in two poor, ill-equipped public schools in our inner city neighborhoods. How was this possible? We as a leadership and a church chose to follow God's vision for us in humble and grateful obedience. The vision statement was further refined to a simpler phrase: A Kingdom resource, Redeeming Destinies. In the church, the people speak of Resource and Redeem because it is so much a part of our spiritual DNA that it overflows like natural speech. Out of the overflow of the vision, life for God is lived!

As the leader, I learned this most important lesson: God puts His vision into *your* heart. He then matches you with a congregation He has chosen and already prepared to do the things He has placed in you, supernaturally arranging for you to come together. Let me say emphatically that vision never comes through a committee or a board. It always comes through a leader. From Abraham to Jesus to Paul, the Scriptures are filled with examples of God giving His people tasks to accomplish which He first gives to a man or a woman of His sovereign choosing.

Once you declare to a group of followers that you have received a vision from God, you are declaring certain powerful truths. You're admitting that your life is now submitted and surrendered to serve God's purposes. You are also saying that you have something to live for which is greater than your own self-interest. And you are choosing to spend your energy, time, love and life in a way that brings glory to God and benefits others. In other words, God's vision for your life and church makes you more like Him, and when people see this it makes it much easier for them to obey Christ and follow you as you serve Him.

As I now lead the Shakaba Global Family, I find myself once again living according to His vision for this wonderful manifestation of His Kingdom. Our vision is this: Share His Kingdom. It is to educate the Church on the the vital importance of living out God's Kingdom whilst at the same time impacting the world with a proper demonstration of His Kingdom. We now live in a post-denominational, post-structural world where half the global population has never heard the name of Jesus, and unless we rise above our local church, denominational and national enclaves to work together under the banner of His Kingdom, we can't possibly hope to reach over three billion people with the Good News of God's love for them.

It is a great task well beyond my human ability to even properly comprehend, but I have learned that unless I receive His vision and live according to His mandate I will never accomplish anything significant for Him, let alone live a satisfying life.

We leaders need to see what God sees and then *rearrange our lives accordingly*.

BAND

2 Timothy 4:11

"Only Luke is with me. Get Mark and bring him with you, for he is useful to me for ministry."

As far back as I can remember, I have wanted to be in a rock and roll band! Truly. I play guitar and can tell you there are few things as gratifying as jamming with a bunch of musicians all rocking out to the same tune, distorted guitar wailing away at silly volume, every note shaking you to the core. It's wonderful. But more than the music, it's the camaraderie developed over months and years of lugging equipment, suffering another cancelled gig, celebrating a great performance or again hanging out together until ludicrous hours of the morning, which transform you from a group into a band and a family. Applying this thinking to work, I have always dreamed of laboring together as a band rather than simply as colleagues checking in and out of the office. This is a hard thing to achieve but when you do, it's like enjoying a little piece of heaven on earth.

It is an established fact that leaders who surround themselves with others better than themselves are much more likely to succeed in their work and goals. The chances they and their ministry will enjoy favor and fruitfulness are magnified just because of this arrangement. It surprises me when I come across leaders still trying to do everything themselves. Not even our Lord Jesus led like that! His first instinct after launching His ministry was to seek His Father for the team of men He would need to help Him fulfil His God ordained purpose and accomplish His God given tasks. These co-laborers became His closest friends and eventually they formed a veritable band of brothers.

To be fruitful in life and leadership, there can be no room for selfish and singular living. As has been famously said, no man is an island. With the constant and growing pressures we face in today's world, we all need a band of brothers or sisters we can rely on, rest with and work alongside to do what we must do. It takes time, energy, understanding and determination to accomplish the building of a band of brothers. The leader cannot be selfish, arrogant or insecure. A leader with these kinds of character flaws may accomplish things in the short term but eventually will run out of respect, support, and followers. There has to be a clearly defined vision in place, which typically is given by the leader and flows into mature collaboration.

Teamwork provides a particular kind of joy and pleasure which going solo never can. The team develops a harmony of thought and action resulting in an easy momentum propelling them forward at a steady pace. They begin to live in movement and everything takes on a new sense of joy and purpose. Although they agree to disagree on some things, there is never conflict. On this note: it always annoys me when a leader tells me conflict is good for a team. Conflict is a military term used to describe war, the natural result of which is always destruction and death. If a leader really believes having war in his team is helpful or productive, I suggest you find another leader or team. Did Jesus ever promote, tolerate or use conflict on His team? Exactly.

Building your "band" requires intentionality. Acknowledge and understand your need for a team. Ask the Lord to send you the teammates He knows you and your work actually need. Then begin a process of looking for the right people. If you're open, prayerful and actively searching, God will make sure you find the right teammates. It takes years of hard work to build and become an effective band, so best to take the time up front to find the right people. They need to have a similar spiritual DNA, believe in your vision and values, fit your culture and desire similar goals. And they need to want friendship and communion.

It's fairly common for leaders to end up working with people they already know. If you're a highly relational person, it's easier to add someone to your team you are already friends with. I do believe this is often the better way to go about building your band as you have the advantage of already knowing your friend's capabilities, value system, work ethic, etc. Of course, God can also add strangers to your band, although this seems to be less typical. In the New Testament, we see how common it was for ministry teams to be built with men who already knew each other, from Jesus to Paul's companions. In today's world, this may be more difficult to do but it is possible.

I encourage you to meditate on the importance of and need for a band of brothers in our life and leadership. We all need others better than ourselves to help us grow and become our best. *When we get this right, everybody wins.*

WHOLE

Proverbs 3:12

" .. the Lord disciplines those he loves, as a father the son he delights in."

Love creates stability and discipline gives security. We all require both in life for balance, effectiveness and meaning. We must raise our children with each of these in good measure and we should lead our church with these too. When we love our children, we communicate to them that they are fully accepted and that they belong to us. Our love assures them of a safe, caring place in this world, a space in which they can freely grow without fear of rejection.

This is an enormously powerful reality for children to be surrounded by and it makes all the difference in how they develop and what kind of adults they grow up to become. It is love that produces stable, free, joyful people. But, it is discipline that produces secure people. When our children learn that there are certain parameters beyond which they should not venture, for their own benefit, it implants security and peace in their souls and minds.

I have had to help many people who were well loved growing up and therefore had a well-developed sense of acceptance, but struggled to make even the simplest decisions. They had never been disciplined and therefore could not grasp the concept of healthy boundaries established for their good and the good of others. Alternately, I have had to lead those who are highly disciplined, hard workers, with a well-defined sense of taking responsibility and functioning effectively within well-defined parameters, but struggling deeply with never feeling good enough for the team or the task at hand. Self-doubt seemed to follow them like a cloud. When I would sit with them privately to try and understand how we could help them, almost always it emerged that they had not enjoyed their parents' love, at least in the tangible ways that children require it.

These truths are highly applicable to life in the ministry too. Leaders who have enjoyed Biblically correct love and discipline turn out to be the healthiest, most respected and most loved leaders of all. They enjoy great fruitfulness in their work because people feel safe, secure and free under their leadership. However, show me an insecure leader, and I will show you someone still struggling with the deep need we all have to be accepted. Or they are frustrated and confused because of lack of clarity, so often brought on by not having enjoyed the caring discipline of loving parents.

Every one of us is broken. Our sin nature guarantees it. But the Holy Spirit desires to heal us of our brokenness and hurt in order to bring us into the fullness of abundant life in Jesus Christ which the Bible tells us it is possible to have through a relationship with Him. The scripture teaches that God disciplines those He loves and parents who turn away from discipline harm their children. I can tell you from firsthand experience this is absolutely true.

The sweetest, most powerful fruit of love and discipline is *confidence*. As our children were growing up, I always said to Delray that the best thing we can instill in our kids is for them to have a deep seated confidence, and the way we do that is to love them immeasurably and discipline them fairly. When we have a God confidence in our spirit, there is very little that can hinder us from accomplishing all that He has for us to be and do.

Love and discipline each require choice. I must *choose* to love others. I must *choose* to discipline those I love. Sometimes, these are the hardest choices to make because not everybody - including ourselves - is easy to love or discipline. But it is very necessary to give and receive both equally. Why? Because the fruit of love and discipline is wholeness. Health. And when something is healthy, it flourishes. A healthy heart, mind and soul is a powerful tool in the hands of God! Health produces fruitfulness, joy and peace. And as leaders, the greatest gift we can offer those who follow us is to be whole and healthy.

FRIEND

James 2:23

"And the scripture was fulfilled that says, "Abraham believed God, and it was credited to him as righteousness," and he was called God's friend."

Reading these words profoundly shaped my life as I understood that the beautiful result of Abraham's obedience to God's call was friendship with Him. It is possible to be friends with God! Considering the environment in which I had been raised, at home and in the Church, this was a radical concept to me. In the Gospel of John 15:13-15 we read, "Greater love has no one than this, that he lay down his life for his friends. You are my friends if you do what I command. I no longer call you servants, because a servant does not know his master's business. Instead, I have called you friends, for everything that I learned from my Father I have made known to you."

Why is it so significant and powerful when Jesus says, "I no longer call you servants ... but have called you friends."? Because Jesus *chose* to call them friends. He didn't have to do that. He could have always kept His relationship to those the Father had given to help Him in

His earthly work more professional, treating them as colleagues rather than close friends. The message we get is clear: friendship involves, includes, shares and results in great growth. Friendship enables entrance into something new. It is the fragrance of His Kingdom.

If Jesus is our example for everything, and we have to make disciples in His name according to His values and practices, then we too have to call those we work with friends. We have to intentionally work at becoming, staying and living as friends. The dictionary defines a friend as a person whom one knows, likes, and trusts: an acquaintance; a person with whom one is allied in a struggle or cause; a comrade; a person attached to another by feelings of affection or personal regard; a person who gives assistance; a patron; a supporter; a person who is on good terms with another; a person who is not hostile.

When we study these words, we see that even an uncaring world - let alone God's kingdom - considers friendship to be vital, significant, necessary and lovely. And yet, in way too many churches, businesses, and families, we see people simply functioning next to each other rather than friends serving closely together.

Almost on a weekly basis, I made sure to regularly spend time with each of our ministry staff, first asking them how they and their families were doing before discussing how their particular area of ministry was fairing. I was very intentional to communicate the message that we are friends first and then colleagues. As we developed a deep affection for each other, trust, respect and care followed very naturally. We enjoyed each another's company and the congregation became aware they were led by a team of friends, not just a bunch of hired hands. Many times visitors commented to me after a service how they had noticed that everybody on the platform seemed to love and respect one other and the church. Our obvious unity and joy was noticeable and infectious. Another enormous benefit was that we were able to speak with each other honestly whenever tensions arose. For the most part, we managed to avoid the gossip, cliques and back biting that comes with simply being employees and colleagues, but instead can be dealt with as friends.

In a similar vein, when guest preachers visited our church we would arrange for them to spend time with each of our ministry staff, usually over a good cup of coffee, away from the church premises. This was very intentional. I knew that if our culture of friendship was to be authentic, it had to permeate all of our lives, not only the ministry staff and congregation. I wanted to ensure that those who preached to our people were also friends of the church and ministered God's Word out of a heart of love and care, not simply as another "preach" on their schedule.

We were amazed to discover how the Lord arranged for our church to have ministry friends from around the world speaking into our lives who could really serve us, challenge us, discipline and bless us, because they were true friends. And like true friends, it didn't matter that we only saw them once or twice per year because the connection was genuine. We avoided the typical trap of a rotating roster of guest speakers with whom the church had no meaningful, growing relationship.

Every Sunday, after opening our worship service with a prayer, I would invite everybody to find two people they had not come to church with and welcome them warmly into God's presence. We quickly became known as a friendly, family style church simply because we included into our spiritual culture regular acts and expressions of friendship and love. Some have said to me that this is personality driven, that I am friendly and that's why we do this, even that it may be negative because we're forcing those who are not naturally "friendly" to have to act so. My response always is that this is the culture of the kingdom: be friendly to everyone and make friends with some. After all, the Bible tells us that Jesus was a friend of sinners, let alone His own followers!

If we are truly servants of Love, surely this is not a complicated concept to grasp or action to put into practice. If I am not naturally friendly, then I must grow to become so, for the sake of His glory and the benefit of those who need to know His friendship in their lives, through me.

I have learned in leadership is that I need at least one true friend in my life. I don't mean my wife... it should be a given that she is my best friend. The Scriptures speak of the one Jesus loved most. Even our Lord needed at least one man He could share His greatest triumphs and difficulties with, as we see demonstrated at the Last

Supper when he leans over to John and tells him that His betrayer is eating at the table with them. And just before He dies on the cross, does He not look at John, His closest friend, and ask him to take care of His mother? I would suggest that if Jesus, as a man, needed a true friend, we would be arrogant and foolish to live our lives choosing to not follow His example.

As I transitioned from leading Calvary Tabernacle Church to leading the Shakaba Global Family, setting aside title and position to begin all over again, I quickly discovered two things: who my real friends are and that because I have real friends, I could do what God had asked of me. Almost all my support, spiritually, emotionally and financially, has come from my friends. I never expected or demanded it, but God has proven Himself faithful through my faithful friends! And as I continue with my new journey, the thing that brings me the greatest joy still is my friendships.

I know for certain that my wealth and worth does not at all lie in the material possessions I have but in the friendships God has added to me over the years. In this regard, I am an outrageously wealthy man.

When I still was a teenager my mother once told me that if in my lifetime I had one true friend I would be luckier than most. Today I am deeply grateful to be able to say I have a number of true friends and consider myself blessed beyond measure.

TODAY

1 Corinthians 9:22

"I have become all things to all men, that I may by all means save some."

It seems as if there is an odd imbalance to this verse, but actually it reveals God's economy when it comes to reaching people with His love. All. All. All. Some. A three to one ratio. "All" is a little word full of big expectations. When it's repeated three times in one sentence and then followed by "some", it would benefit us to pause and understand what the Apostle Paul is saying to us.

Paul powerfully accomplished his mandate for God amongst various cultures, including the Jews, Greeks and Romans. He spoke several languages. He travelled much. He worked both in the church and the business worlds, being highly fruitful in each. If he was alive today, we'd say he's a globalist, culturalist, entrepreneur and thought leader. In a word, relevant.

As leaders, it is vital to be in touch with where people actually live in order to reach them effectively. It takes intentionality to remain relevant: determination, desire, effort and practice. It still confounds me when I meet leaders who tell me they never watch TV, go to the movies, attend concerts or travel. They wait for the people they say they want to reach with God's love to come to them instead of going to those dear people, as Paul did. It takes a firm decision to lead like Jesus and Paul led, serving those we care for from within their living space rather than waiting for them to come to ours.

I am not saying every full-time minister leader should quit their ministry job and get a "secular" job. I am saying they should find ways to live among the people they serve and those they're wanting to reach for God. Maybe your "all", in God's intentions for your life, includes a complete change from where you find yourself today. You can join Meetup groups, a sports team, start a small business on the side.. the opportunities are endless. After years of working in the church world, I now run my own Imaging Studio, ZOmedia, and wouldn't change it for anything. I am meeting people who have never set foot in a church and forming stimulating friendships which are a blessing to me as much as I am to them. I am learning firsthand what people outside the church really think and feel about God, spirituality and life. It's making me a much better leader and more fruitful Christian.

It's been tough starting over again in an unfamiliar world. However, I'm learning that God listens to every prayer we pray and doesn't forget, like we do. My life today is God answering earnest prayers I prayed years ago to be relevant, reaching people in their own context. Of course I didn't anticipate I would end up in the business world, running my own business! I imagined I'd be a typical missionary in some far off land. I am loving this new, scary, challenging, journey. Most importantly, I have discovered a level of love for those who don't yet know their Savior I had not experienced before and I'm growing as a person and a Christian in so many new ways.

Throughout my Christian life I have made a point of having fiends both inside and outside the church. I always want to understand the prevailing culture so I can reach it effectively. Even when working full-time in the ministry, I kept doing graphic design work on the side. I'm a movie junkie. I read a lot: magazines, comics, newspapers, books, etc. I asked our kids to keep me relevant: Joel is my music manager and Bianca is my my fashion manager. All this for the benefit of staying relevant in an ever changing world.

What strikes me about the verse above is that Paul became all things to all men, not some things to some men. He chose and changed. He adapted. He did whatever was necessary, short of sinning, to reach those who didn't yet know Christ personally because he cared that much. And as a leader setting the example for his fellow leaders and the next generation coming after them, he was demonstrating how leaders grow the Kingdom of God. He was fully aware of the need to be relevant and rearranged his life accordingly.

"All" means everything!

I wonder what things Paul did that aren't recorded in the Scriptures which are included in his "all". All things, to all men. His "all" must have

covered food, drink, clothing, language, activity, etc. In my own leadership journey I have sought to follow Paul's example and it has turned out to be a fantastic way of living for Christ. When I'm doing an Emerging Leadership Conference in Bulgaria, it means staying up until 2AM talking through what had been shared that evening, usually in a smoke filled restaurant with wonderfully unsavory characters all around us. They don't have "Christian" coffee shops so we happily eat at the kind of places where regular Bulgarians enjoy food and drink.

In India, it's super spicy food, lots of driving, extreme heat and no privacy. People everywhere, all the time. Finland is the opposite of that: lakes, more lakes, and sauna's. And cold weather. Screamingly funny people with the best sense of humor I've encountered in any culture. Not many hugs though and I'm a big time hugger, so you can imagine the response I received after publicly hugging my translator and kissing him on the cheek in church!

In each of the various settings God has used me to serve Him, I had to choose to adapt in order to relevantly reach and help those I was serving. The onus was on me, not them.

I have countless wonderful stories to share but the point is this: as a leader, you choose to become something you are not yet in order to reach "some". It may cause you discomfort, frustration, irritation and even pain. But it will also help you grow, live a far more interesting life and be way more fruitful than if you remained where you "live" right now. But it is a choice you must make. Relevance doesn't just happen on its own - it takes intention and effort born out of compassion.

Jack Hayford once said the Holy Spirit showed him as a young leader that in his lifetime he would go through four generational shifts, and it was his responsibility to grow and adjust in order to be relevant in each new generation. He shared how difficult that was for him because he, like so many others, doesn't naturally enjoy change. He felt that he was already good enough. For example, he grew up listening to old style choral music but now in his later life was enjoying quality rap and hip hop. He chose to educate himself on rap music because

God was adding so many young adults and teens to his church that he wanted to speak with them in ways they could relate to. One of those things was their music. Obviously he didn't have to become a rapper, but he did have to become open to listen to, understand and appreciate a form of art he wasn't naturally drawn to. He, like Paul, was still becoming all things to all men in order to reach some.

He was staying *relevant*.

True

Living authentically

I once read the amazing story of how the incomparable Michelangelo and other sculptors of his day would take their creations down to the public marketplace to sell, and walking before them would be a young man yelling, "Sensa Cera! Sensa Cera!" Translated from its original Latin, it means "without wax". Sculpting a human figure out of a solid piece of marble is incredibly difficult and arduous work requiring much planning, testing, and preparation. The artist must visualize the completed work in his mind before he begins to chip away at the roughly shaped rock standing before him, one chisel strike at a time.

Sometimes, as he was sculpting, the artist would make a mistake and create a crack or fracture where there shouldn't be one. His assistant would then cover the fault with some high-quality wax in order to conceal the error. The problem was that when they took the sculpture to an outdoor market to sell, the hot sun would beat down on the sculpture, melt the wax, and reveal the flaws contained within the work. The piece would lose much value and the potential buyer would either move on or attempt to bargain for a cheaper price.

On hearing the words "Sensa cera!", prospective buyers would immediately appreciate that the work of art they were thinking of purchasing was perfectly created from a single piece of marble, free of any cracks or scuff marks from the artist's chisel and hammer. Imagine their hearts racing as they beheld the beauty of the piece before them, knowing that over time, apart from being lovely to behold, it would escalate in value and therefore make a good investment. The finest sculptors were those ablest to produce works without wax. Their labor was authentic, the fruit of grand imagination, hard work, and pure skill.

Our world is looking for leaders who can cry out, "Sensa cera!" True "artists" who take great care and pride in their labor for God. Who show great imagination, work hard, and love their calling. But unfortunately, our world today has too many wax filled leaders. Men and women hiding character flaws, sinful living and sheer disregard for God's Kingdom or His people, looking to take advantage of those who follow them. They promote themselves as honest artists but are in fact spiritual frauds. I am not referring only to those leaders who are dishonest and selfish, but also those who lack imagination, passion and courage to create something beautiful for God which brings Him glory.

I am not saying we must be perfect! All of us are filled with cracks and marks and scrapes because we are all born sinners. I am saying however that each of us has the choice to live an authentic, honest life, free of scheming, hiding, and trickery. It takes a lot of very hard, intentional work, daily, to live this kind of authentic life. Waxless is tough. The sun of adversity, criticism, accountability, etc., is always beating down on our "sculpture" to see if we have wax covering our cracks. And, in each of our lives, there are two sculptures we are always working on: ourselves and our work. And the task is never done.

One powerful way to achieve "Sensa cera!" is to befriend the "Michelangelo's" of your particular world. We all need mentors and examples to follow who can help us on our "waxless" journey. You really need only one or two of these. Better to walk deeply with one teacher than on a surface level with several. Imagine the benefit Michelangelo's students had of learning from a true master who had already made his mistakes? It's the same for us today.. find a great example of authenticity, befriend them and learn under their tutelage.

As a leader, I somehow knew instinctively that it is always better to live transparently and honestly before your followers than it is to try and hide from them. It is true that too many times I revealed too much of myself and my work too publicly, and I paid dearly for that immaturity, as did my family. I have had to apologize too many times to count to my loved ones for sharing too much information with the public, sometimes even in inappropriate ways.

Let me share a personal example of immature "Sensa cera!". The first time I told our church that Delray and I had a major argument and I had treated her unfairly, instead of showing appreciation, she and our kids were angry and disappointed with me. I thought it would help the congregation to know their leader was "normal" and a "regular" guy, but it actually caused some of them to be confused because they assumed we had a nearly perfect marriage. Delray told me that if I had first checked with her whether I could share our story or not, she probably would have given me permission and would have even helped me write it out. So, lesson learned! A positive result was that many people did in fact approach us both over the following weeks, expressing their relief and even joy at hearing that the beloved leader could fail just like them, and was authentically sharing his life with them. Living "Sensa cera" is always better, even if it is costlier.

Now a more positive example. When our congregation was faced with difficult situations where sharing the facts of a given issue might cause alarm or resistance, I always chose to share truth in a loving, clear manner, believing the end result would be healthier for us all. At our annual business meetings and during special voting sessions, we went out of our way to ensure nothing was hidden or covered over by our leadership team. We faced difficult questions honestly, face to face, in an open forum, and when we made mistakes, we acknowledged our fault and apologized accordingly. The congregation was happy to follow our leadership because we were transparent and authentic. That was the road we chose and we walked it to the best of our ability. It began with me as the leader, as these things typically do.

Ultimately, living authentically isn't a single decision you make but a series of many, many smaller choices made daily. It's a never ending journey you cannot avoid which leads you higher and higher up the mountain of Truth. Although the travel may be more strenuous the higher you climb, the view is also grander with each passing step.

CERTAIN

Philippians 1:25

"And being confident of this, I know that I shall remain and continue with you all for your progress and joy of faith .."

Confidence is a wonderful servant and insecurity a miserable master. Confidence plays a major role in our everyday lives. I am not speaking of human confidence based on skill, talent or charm. I am referring to a God given confidence emanating from the very depths of my spirit, shaping my heart, mind and soul.

Midway through my forties, I had a life changing experience. One morning after waking up, I stumbled through to the bathroom in a half awake, half asleep state and stood staring at my reflection in the bathroom mirror. After splashing some water on my face to try and properly wake up, as I stood there like a zombie, my mouth opened and I heard the words, "I like you .. I really like you." It was a little confusing and shocking. Then I suddenly realized it wasn't me speaking but the Lord Jesus using my own voice to tell me that He likes me. That He doesn't only love me - He loves everyone, after all - but that He *likes* me. I began crying as I felt my insides begin to shake, so I went downstairs in order not to wake up Delray. The thought came to to me to read Psalm 139 in the Bible. Slowly and surely, the Holy Spirit gave me understanding that the Father had made me in my mother's womb to have the personality I had. My serious spirit. My enquiring mind. My creative and adventurous soul. My loving nature. And my somewhat uniquely odd sense of humor. My tears gave way to feelings of profound joy and freedom as I realized that Jesus had chosen to like me and He even enjoyed me! It was a transformative experience and on certain levels my life really began that day.

I began studying Psalm 139 in depth and quickly discovered that in reality it was studying me. What I mean is that this Psalm became a mirror reflecting me back to myself and the image I saw was not who I was used to looking at. Underneath the exterior of the self-made Lorenzo was a God created Lorenzo He was daily transforming into His image. The Bible teaches that the Truth will set you free and that is exactly what happened to me. I began to enjoy my walk with the Lord as never before, this new found freedom enabling me to be bolder for Him. In essence, I had gained a God confidence. I now see that He had been working this truth into my heart for many years but on that day when I looked in the mirror and heard His voice, He fully opened the door enabling me to step into the wonderful, powerful confidence which only He can give to us. My leadership changed profoundly as I now led with a certainty, clarity and strength I had not known before. My family, friends and the congregation all noticed that something had changed in me. I no longer apologized for myself: my way of thinking, my humor, my affectionate behavior, and my very public declaration of love for Christ. I now say to leaders all over the world: never apologize for who God made you to be and for what He made you to do. Be yourself! Your God designed self.

Confidence enables secure, responsible and effective leadership. You are able to give the direction those following you require. It empowers you to make decisions more quickly and not be double minded. It also facilitates saying "No" to the wrong things and "Yes" to the right things.

In Joshua 1, we see Joshua leading the Israelites across the Jordan river into the Promised Land with confidence after God had spoken to him, reminding him to be strong and courageous, rejecting fear and doubt. Joshua could be certain as he issued commands to his leaders to prepare to move out because He had a God confidence in him. He knew God had spoken and was sure God was with them.

One of the biggest difficulties I faced as a leader was working under and with insecure leaders. Men and women who lack God confidence and instead rely on their own character and abilities to lead. To be frank, it is the one aspect of leadership I now most dislike. I have been so mistreated and let down by insecure leaders that today I won't work with or place myself under the authority of such people. Insecurity is very destructive. It immobilizes leaders. It causes them to be petty and punitive. It fosters jealousy, smallness, control and division. I fully understand that every human being, as a result of our sin nature, has some level of insecurity in them, so I am referring to leaders who know they are inherently insecure yet refuse to allow the Holy Spirit to heal and deliver them of this weakness in their life. Instead, they make excuses for their behavior and insist on leading through their smallness.

True confidence for life and leadership comes from personally knowing, loving and serving the One who made you, and from humbly, joyously and freely expressing your true self to His glory. On so many different and important levels, the best thing you can give your family, friends and followers is true, Godly confidence.

When you are confident in God, *anything is possible!*

THREAD

We all have a life filter in us

It's there .. we just need to discover it and develop it to the potential God intended. It is like an invisible thread running through everything we are and do.

For me and Delray, our life filter - our LifeThread - has always been dignity. To this day, few things in life anger me more than people acting rudely, treating others with disrespect. Rudeness not only shows disregard for those God created and loves, it reveals an arrogant spirit and contemptuous heart, both of which are offensive to God and should be to us as well. Treating others with dignity, on the other hand, reveals the complete opposite attitude and recognizes the value, beauty and importance of those God so lovingly crafted and blessed the world with. Dignity is one of love's keys. It closes doors of hate and opens doors of acceptance, encouragement, joy, and purpose.

This LifeThread - our filter - is deeply embedded in our soul and psyche, finding myriad ways of manifesting itself daily through our lives. It pushes and pulls us into joy, meaning, courage, action, and purpose. It is invisible yet tangible, silent yet shouts loudly, hidden but ever present. It is, in essence, the very fabric of our nature, character and practice. We cannot avoid it but we can choose to ignore it. We cannot live without it but we can try to avoid it. Ultimately, we choose either to give it the freedom to fully express itself or to be bound, and even silenced.

When Delray and I lived in South Africa, during the 1980's we were deeply involved in the ministry of reconciling white and black Christians to one another, primarily through the vehicle of music. One of our church elders, Dave Van Zyl, an amazing man of God and highly successful and influential businessman, asked Delray to bring together a multi-racial singing group to perform a few songs at the annual Christian Businessmen's Fellowship Christmas breakfast. She immediately contacted the leadership of a local African church in the nearby township of Alexandria and they kindly agreed to send us a few of their finest choir members. Within a couple of weeks, the Jabulani Team was born and the rest is history.

Over the course of several years, God used us in many ways to reconcile previously estranged black and white people. We served in churches, in townships, at conferences, at home and on the road, on national TV and radio stations, to bring the message of dignity to a nation at war with itself and its neighbors. It was a dangerous, exhausting, rewarding and exhilarating journey. We felt uncertain yet confident that He had chosen us to bring His Kingdom character to our country. The thread which bound us so tightly together was dignity. At the time, none of us properly understood that God was putting together this incredibly beautiful, powerful and significant ministry to serve His purposes for bringing healing to South Africa.

The reason God chose Dave Van Zyl and us is because we both had the Kingdom nature of God's dignity running through our spiritual veins. God knew that the way to break down walls of separation and to level mountains of racism was by gathering together His servants who would treat one another with the respect only Jesus can impart to us all because of His victorious work on the Cross. It wasn't enough to just meet and sing together. We had to learn to communicate with each other, to listen with open hearts, serve with open hands and to trust with generous spirits. We had to treat each other as Christ treated us, with dignity. And the Lord knew he could entrust us with the task because it was He who put the LifeThread of dignity in each of us. And then, at the right moment in history, He joined us together to accomplish a particular task which required that LifeThread to manifest and be lived out.

I am humbled and joyful to be able to say that the life filter of dignity is stronger in our lives today than ever before. Your LifeThread is like a mighty tree which grows taller each year, it's roots digging deeper, it's seeds spreading further as it increases in size and influence. If you nourish it, you will become the person and tool in God's hands to accomplish His Kingdom purposes to the measure He intended when He first infused your LifeThread into you in your mother's womb.

What is your life filter? What is the thread that runs through your existence? Are you preparing yourself for the moment in history when God will require you to entrust your LifeThread into His mighty hands so He can accomplish His great purposes through you, in His time, for His glory? It is better to seek to understand these things before you are required to serve so that when the time comes, you are ready to make a difference in as full a measure as possible.

The lesson for us all is that we are driven by invisible forces seated deep within our beings. These forces make us who we are and direct what we do. But it is we who determine whether to walk with them as friends or silence them as enemies.

MEASURE

Living within your Grace Space

There are some questions in the Kingdom of God I find quite perplexing and difficult to understand. One of them is this: why is it that no matter how hard they pray, study and work, some leaders are not able to grow their church or ministry beyond a certain point? They attend the latest and greatest leadership seminars and conferences; they read the "must have" books; they visit larger, growing churches to learn what they could possibly do to improve and grow their ministry. But it seems that regardless of what they do, their ministry doesn't grow beyond a certain point. I think of the good men and women I know who do everything right but what I have written above is their story. Although I certainly do not claim to have the answer, I think I may have some insight into this question which I share in the hope that it will help, encourage and even free you.

I had the privilege and joy of being the Lead Minister at Calvary Tabernacle Church in Schenectady, NY, for fifteen years. When I arrived at the church, they had just been through a very painful split and the remaining congregation, approximately a hundred and twenty strong, were in need of much care and healthy leadership. Years later, when the leadership team and I announced to the church that in September 2012 that I would be stepping down from my leadership role to pursue the Father's mandate for me to lead the Shakaba Global Family, we were averaging seven hundred worshippers at our Sunday morning worship service. Finances were very healthy, our Missions program was humming, and we had a quality staff and leadership team. Most importantly, we were deeply involved in our local community, serving the poor. And our worship was of a depth and quality I still have not experienced anywhere else.

For nearly two years before I left, our numbers had plateaued and although my preaching was better than ever and our team was attending some of the right church growth conferences, we just couldn't seem to grow beyond a certain point. If you ask the leaders who are now in charge (and the Staff) I'm sure they, as I do, will have many opinions on why this was the case. However, after all is said and done, I think it is simply this: I had reached my God given measure for growing that church. When a leader reaches their God given measure - what I also call their "grace space" – no matter what they attempt in order to grow beyond that measure, they cannot because the Lord won't move you beyond the parameters He has already established for you.

To better understand this, let's look at the life of the Apostle Paul. In the book of Romans 12:3 & 6, Paul says, "For I say, through the grace given to me, to everyone who is among you, not to think of himself more highly than he ought to think, but to think soberly, as God has dealt to each one a measure of faith. Having then gifts differing according to the grace that is given to us, let us use them." Again in 2 Corinthians 10:13, Paul refers to his measure when he says, "We, however, will not boast beyond measure, but within the limits of the sphere which God appointed us." Limits. Sphere. What interesting language. He teaches us that God has given to each one of us a measure of faith, a measure of grace, and a sphere, or scope, of service. Faith (in every sense of the word) to believe, know and trust Him for the task, grace to do it, and a sphere to do it in, within limits He has set. In Ephesians 4:7 we read, "But to each one of us grace was given according to the measure of Christ's gift."

Our individual measure is a manifestation of a portion of Christ's own measure as He determines. In other words, Christ decides the purpose and size of His gift (actually, Himself) in us and its expression through us.

We cannot change the measure God has given us or the scope of the work He has called us to. What we can and must do is discover it, understand it, and then live it out in the Spirit's power, to the fullest expression possible.

Paul even goes so far as to make himself incredibly vulnerable for the sake of helping other leaders to understand the importance of serving within your measure when he confesses that God had a plan to ensure Paul didn't exceed his measure. And it isn't a pleasant plan. Paul admits in 2 Corinthians 12:7, "And lest I should be exalted above measure by the abundance of the revelations, a thorn in the flesh was given to me, a messenger of Satan to buffet me, lest I be exalted above measure." He repeats the words "lest I should be exalted above my measure" as if to stress the importance of this message. Can you imagine? God is allowing Paul to suffer in order to prevent him going beyond his measure. Why? because it would be harmful to Paul for him to do so. Either he would boast and God would need to humble him, or he would endanger himself and possibly derail his ministry, thereby never fulfilling his God given measure. In other words, he and the Kingdom would suffer loss, not to mention the souls that would not be saved due to his overreaching.

When I operated within the measure of faith, grace and scope the Father had ordained for me, all was well and we were favored by God. However, when I attempted to operate outside of my grace space, things didn't go well for me or those I was serving. So much of who I am and what I do is included in my God given measure. I am by nature loving, innovative, inspirational, exploring and constantly in need of a lot of stimulation. This was reflected in the culture of our church. We were loving, constantly updating everything, highly missional, etc. Why? Because God's measure for me shapes those he has included in my scope of ministry. I was supposed to grow the church to seven hundred and then hand it over to someone with a larger measure who could take it further. God's measure in me helped us become a creative, missional church with a highly relational culture. That's what Calvary Tabernacle needed at that stage of their development in God. In a similar way my God given measure will shape the Shakaba Global Family in ways they need to be shaped. And one day, once I reach my measure in this mandate for God, I will need to hand them over to someone with a larger measure who can grow it further.

Consider this for a moment: in all Creation, the only One with a perfect and unlimited measure is our Lord Jesus Christ. And right now, through the Holy Spirit, by His Father's will, He is working out His measure through each and every one of us in order to bring as many people as possible to know His Father and be with Him for eternity. The issue is not the size of the measure but whether you and I are expressing it correctly and fully. I pray you will take the time to discover and understand your measure. And that you will have the humility and courage to accept it, whether it be large or small. One thing you can rest and rejoice in is the assurance that our loving Father created you in your mother's womb with perfect knowledge to be able to contain the measure He would be giving you for your life of service to Him. Your measure is not a mystery to be solved but a wonder to be uncovered and displayed for His glory and the good of others.

Some thoughts to ponder:
A leader's measure covers those serving with and under him. When that covering is removed, the individual measures of others are revealed for their true scope.

A leader with a measure smaller than someone under him will limit and frustrate their measure. Either he needs to make room for the larger measure or he must remove himself. And it's also true that any leader replacing the one moving on will "re-scope" the ministry to their own measure.

As long as you operate within your God given measure, you will have whatever is required for your God given task.

Does a church have a measure? No, measures are given to people. Tasks are given to churches, and the Father then matches the measure with the task.

BETTER

Romans 8:29

".. to be conformed to the image of his Son .."

In the Kingdom of God, everything is aimed at one particular goal: to conform us into the image of Jesus Christ. In the verse above, we learn that the Father's chief aim for every one of us is that we become like His Son. This is the reason He teaches, trains and tests us. His great eternal vision is Heaven filled with those who are conformed to Christ's perfect image. What a privilege to be one of those whom God has on this journey!

Of course, along the way we get some things right and other things wrong. Too many to count! But the sum of all our experiences make us who we are, so it is beneficial to learn from both the good and the bad, the right and the wrong, the wise and the foolish. Below I have chosen to share the main things I got right and wrong as a leader. I hope my honesty helps you in your journey to being transformed into Christ's image.

The main thing I got right as a leader: Team leadership

A younger leader once asked me if I had a secret to our "success" as a rapidly growing church and ministry. Without hesitation, I replied, "Find people better than you and convince them to work with you!" This still holds true for me today. It takes a couple of main things to be able to get this right. The first is fully understanding and appreciating that your identity is in Jesus Christ and not in your abilities, personality, etc. Once the Holy Spirit made this real to me, I lost all need to prove anything to myself or others, and I also lost all fear of pleasing people. This freed me to pursue His calling and purposes with passion and peace.

The second is loss of insecurity. You can't hire people better than you if you're insecure as a person, otherwise when those around you perform better or become more popular, it'll make you jealous and cause you to become punitive. You then lead out of fear, resentment, jealousy or unforgiveness. I had this happen with someone I hired to work with me - I thought I knew them but it soon became apparent that wasn't the case. I spent quite a while wondering if I did something wrong, but once I moved on to the next mandate God had for me, I understood that it's this leader's deep insecurity that was mostly the issue. However, as the leader, I have to take responsibility for hiring them.

Please appreciate that I am not insecure not because I'm a good leader but because once I was born again and received Christ as my personal Savior, He powerfully transformed me to become who I am today. I was a worrying child and a very angry young man, but once He came into my life, by the power of the Holy Spirit He transformed me at the deepest level. We are never free to say: this is who I am, take it or leave it. No, *because* we are leaders, we *must* allow Him full and free access to remake us into who He always intended us to be!

Due to this transformation, it became effortless for me to eagerly look for and hire better people than me. When you do this, everybody wins. They are happy to function in their God given gifting, you can focus on what you're supposed to be doing, and those you serve together benefit immeasurably. If we truly desire to be like Christ in every way, then as leaders, we have to follow His example of leadership. The first thing He did once he began His ministry journey was to enlist the help of twelve other men. Think about this: Peter was a better fisherman than Jesus, so he understood the need for teamwork in order to successfully catch fish. Even Christ was not beyond joining others to His vision who were better than Him in their given area of expertise.

The main thing I got wrong as a leader: being too kind

By far, the one thing I got wrong more than anything else was being too kind. By nature, I am a very friendly, amiable and caring person, hence my deep focus on friendship. Nothing pleases me more than bringing joy to others, especially those close to me. This proved to be both my greatest asset and weakness. Let me explain what I mean. The Scriptures tell us that prophecy is given to the church for encouragement, correction, and direction. We each need all three elements in our lives and work. With anybody who served under my leadership, I was very encouraging and mostly focused on helping people find their direction, or sweet spot, in life and ministry. I loved doing it and found it highly rewarding. But I was imbalanced, because where I lacked was in giving correction when it became necessary. I didn't understand, or chose to not properly understand, the crucial need for this aspect of leadership. After all, the
Scripture does make it clear that all three elements are needed for raising mature followers of Christ able to fruitfully lead His people.

Some of the reason for this failure in leadership stems from my difficult and painful upbringing, where I had to learn from a very early age to find friends outside my home. This need for friendship defined my life in profound ways. Positively, it taught me how to communicate effectively and live fearlessly. Negatively, it made me needy of the approval of others, which some people readily abused, from family members to work and ministry colleagues. However, for the sake of God's glory, I have to state for the record that by my early thirties, the neediness disappeared, replaced by choice. I chose to rely on Christ's full acceptance of me and have lived for years choosing to be friendly, making friends, even whilst knowing that some of those might cause me great pain.

Being too kind can sometimes hurt you, the person you think you're helping by not speaking the truth in love to them when they require it, and those you both are

serving. For example, some leaders serving under me wanted to change their roles from those for which they had been hired, and I agreed to allow it as I wanted to be kind to them. I allowed their personal preference to supersede what was necessary for the wider congregation and to fulfil our God given vision. What resulted was frustration in the congregation and a growing sense of entitlement in the individual's concerned. This is one example of being too kind. Instead of pointing out that they had been hired to fulfil a particular area of need in the church, I made a poor choice because I wanted *them* to be happy.

I have been privileged to serve alongside some world-class leaders. I thoroughly enjoyed most of my time in that Kingdom role, and more than anything else, the Lord used the Pastoral Ministry to shape me into Christ's image. The reality is we cannot avoid being who we are. However, with God's guidance and enablement, and a lot of hard work, we can grow into the leader he designed us to be.

CONCLUSION

Thank you!

It has been both joyful and painful to write this book. Before I began, I decided I would be honest and not sugarcoat my journey to make me look like a near perfect leader. As I have read and re-read it many times, I corrected the earlier transcripts to be less idyllic and more accurately reflect both my fruitful times and failures.

I imagine there are a number of these lessons which resonated with your own journey and there are some you have yet to experience. Hopefully, this book has given you food for meditation and prayer. It is my sincere hope that these pages have brought you courage and freedom to live your God-given uniqueness in meaningful, joyful ways resulting in glory to the Father and good to man.

Life is an immeasurably precious gift. Lessons are soulmates. May both be your constant companions.

With love and thanks,

Lorenzo Agnes

Lorenzo

If you enjoyed this book, you may be interested in more of my writings, art, design and photography. Please take a moment to visit me at lorenzoagnes.com

Thanks again for purchasing Lingering Lessons on Life & Leadership!

Lorenzo Agnes

www.ingramcontent.com/pod-product-compliance
Lightning Source LLC
Chambersburg PA
CBHW060356190526
45169CB00002B/618